A DAY IN AN ECOSYSTEM

24 HOURS IN THE TAIGA

ALICIA Z. KLEPEIS

Cavendish
Square
New York

Published in 2018 by Cavendish Square Publishing, LLC
243 5th Avenue, Suite 136, New York, NY 10016

First Edition

Website: cavendishsq.com

This publication represents the opinions and views of the author based on his or her personal experience, knowledge, and research. The information in this book serves as a general guide only. The author and publisher have used their best efforts in preparing this book and disclaim liability rising directly or indirectly from the use and application of this book.

CPSIA Compliance Information: Batch #CS17CSQ

All websites were available and accurate when this book was sent to press.

Library of Congress Cataloging-in-Publication Data

Names: Klepeis, Alicia, 1971-
Title: 24 hours in the taiga / Alicia Z. Klepeis.
Other titles: Twenty-four hours in the taiga
Description: New York : Cavendish Square Publishing, [2018] | Series: A day in an ecosystem | Includes index.
Identifiers: LCCN 2016057667 (print) | LCCN 2016059342 (ebook) | ISBN 9781502624840 (library bound) | ISBN 9781502624857 (E-book)
Subjects: LCSH: Taiga ecology. | Permafrost forest ecology. | Taigas. | Forests and forestry--Northern Hemisphere.
Classification: LCC QK938.T34 K54 2018 (print) | LCC QK938.T34 (ebook) | DDC 577.3/7--dc23
LC record available at HYPERLINK "https://lccn.loc.gov/2016057667" https://lccn.loc.gov/2016057667

Editorial Director: David McNamara
Editor: Fletcher Doyle
Copy Editor: Rebecca Rohan
Associate Art Director: Amy Greenan
Designer: Stephanie Flecha
Production Coordinator: Karol Szymczuk
Photo Research: J8 Media

Printed in the United States of America

CONTENTS

DAWN

THE sun is just coming up as you step out of your cabin. It's very early in the morning. You rub your eyes as you try to wake yourself. Just ahead, you see a fire blazing in the firepit. Your guide, a Canadian science teacher, calls to you. As you stumble along the path, you step on a pinecone. It makes a crunching sound. The air smells like pine needles. It reminds you of a Christmas tree.

When you arrive by the fire, you are delighted. Your guide has made you hot cocoa. Back home, you'd never be drinking a hot beverage in July. But in the early morning hours, it's chilly here. Where are you? In the Canadian taiga.

The word "taiga" is Russian. It refers to a type of forest found in the world's cold, subarctic regions. Taiga lies just south of the Arctic Circle in the Northern Hemisphere. Alaska and Canada have large stretches of taiga. So do Scandinavia and Russia. The Canadian taiga stretches more than 3,100 miles (5,000 kilometers) from the Yukon in the west to Newfoundland and Labrador in the east.

A boreal chickadee stands amidst a pile of seeds. These birds often come to people's birdfeeders.

This snowshoe hare displays its summer coloration. The hare is in Alaska's Denali National Park.

Another name for taiga is **boreal** forest. This northern forest takes its name from Boreas, the Greek god of the north wind. Sometimes this kind of forest is swampy. It is largely made up of **conifers**, also called evergreen trees. The cone shape of these trees comes in handy in winter. Why? The snow can just fall off the trees so the branches don't break under the weight of the snow. But there's no snow now—it's summertime.

You zip up your hoodie and sit on a stump. A symphony of birdcalls surrounds you. "Chick-a-dee-dee!" A scratchy birdcall sounds familiar to you. Your guide points to the branch of a nearby spruce tree. You'd expected to see the black-and-white head of a black-capped chickadee. But when you get out your binoculars, it's a boreal chickadee instead. In the dim light, you can just make out its tiny brown head. These birds store up spruce seeds and insect **larvae** for the winter. Food can be scarce in the taiga if you don't plan ahead.

Many different plants and animals live in boreal forests. Squirrels and raccoons make their homes here. Different fish swim in the lakes and rivers. Huge numbers of birds stop in boreal forests as they **migrate** from their summer to their winter homes. The taiga has a variety of plants from mosses to flowers to shrubs. Some **species** are found only in the taiga.

The Canadian taiga is home to many kinds of plants, birds, fish, and other animals. Every one depends on the others for its survival. They are part of an **ecosystem**. An ecosystem includes both the living things that interact in a particular area and their environment (such as the nonliving parts like water, soil, sunlight, and so on).

After eating some bread and cheese, you are ready to head out on the trail. The sky is brightening. A snowshoe hare pops into view from under a shrub. It nibbles some berries. Its summer fur is grayish-brown. This helps it blend in with its surroundings. In the winter, its fur will be white to blend in with the snow. Its back feet are long and covered with fur. This gives it traction on ice and snow. **Camouflage** is essential for snowshoe hares. Many animals, like coyotes, foxes, and lynx, **prey** on them.

After the hare runs off, you can't wait to find out what you will see farther down the trail.

A Canada lynx crouches on a rock during the warmer months. It may be in the process of stalking prey.

CANADA LYNX

The main source of food for the Canada lynx is the snowshoe hare. This cat stands about 20 inches (50 centimeters) tall at the shoulder. Its long ear **tufts** and short, black-tipped tail help people identify it. These lynx avoid contact with humans and are very hard to spy.

MORNING

BE sure to gather your supplies for the day. You'll need a notebook to make sketches of the plants and animals you see for your scouting badge. The camera and sound recorder on your phone will come in handy, too, though it's unlikely you'll have coverage to make calls in this wilderness.

You put on your rubber boots. The taiga has lots of lakes, ponds, and marshes. Your guide says that not far down the trail is a **muskeg**. Is that some kind of animal? Nope, a muskeg is a kind of swamp or **bog**. The wet land of a muskeg is often covered with mosses and other plant life. It looks like solid ground. If you weren't paying attention, it would be easy to end up ankle-deep in water here. Muskegs are very common in boreal forests.

When you arrive at the muskeg, you notice something. Around its edge, black spruce and tamarack trees are growing. Muskegs can be found in depressions made by glaciers thousands of years ago. The soil here is

A variety of small plants and mosses surround a muskeg in Canada's Yukon Territory.

This close-up shows the tiny, bright green leaves of sphagnum moss that form a mat over ground that is very wet.

poorly drained. You kneel down and find a spongy mat below your feet. Sphagnum moss (sometimes called peat moss) is growing here. It's soft and super-thick when you touch it. Your guide mentions that peat mosses can absorb water better than a sponge. And some Native American groups, like the Woods Cree, treated diaper rash with a species of sphagnum called rusty peat moss. Why? It is absorbent and has antiseptic qualities.

Mosses aren't the only plants you find in the muskeg. You also see some **sedges** growing here. These grasslike plants like wet ground. Their

The top of a black spruce in Canada's Kouchibouguac National Park is laden with cones.

flowers are so tiny you can barely see them. You create a quick sketch and put your notebook back into your bag. Following in your guide's footsteps, you wander among the black spruce trees. Their bark is scaly and greenish-brown in color. Small, purplish seed cones hang off these trees.

Like these spruces, most of the trees in the boreal forest are conifers. They have needles instead of broad leaves. Their seeds grow inside of cones that protect them. Conifers have adapted to survive the tough weather conditions of the taiga. Winters are long and cold, and the summers are short. Coniferous trees are able to use their dark, triangle-shaped needles to absorb as much of the sun's light as possible. They use the sunlight to make their own food in a process called **photosynthesis**. This process lets oxygen

A stoat looks out over its habitat, which is covered in blooming wildflowers.

ERMINE

Much like the snowshoe hare, the ermine also changes its fur according to the time of year. In summer, the ermine's fur is chocolate brown; its winter coat is white. This creature is also known as a stoat or a short-tailed weasel. Ermine have long bodies, short legs, and long necks. These predators eat small mammals, birds, eggs, fish, and insects (among other foods).

off into the air, which animals need to breathe.

In the distance you see what looks like a small lake. You can't tell exactly how far away it is. All of a sudden, you hear a strange noise. It sounds a bit like someone is yodeling. You look at your guide and he smiles. That weird sound actually has a fancy name: a tremolo. What is making the noise? A common loon. Loons make the wavering tremolo sound if they are alarmed or if they want to announce their presence.

Eventually you arrive at the lake and can see the loons for yourself. Between 28 and 36 inches (71 to 91 cm) long, they are bigger than you'd expected. You look through your binoculars to see them up close. The loon you focus on has a black head and neck. Its back is black with white spots. Out of nowhere, another loon flies into view. It dives into the water, fast as a torpedo. In seconds, it emerges from the water with a wriggling fish. The loon swallows the fish headfirst, in one gulp! Loons eat a variety of prey from minnows and perch to frogs.

Canada's boreal forests are home to around 130 fish species. Most of these fish, like sticklebacks and minnows, are small. But there are some larger fish. Lake trout, yellow perch, and burbot are some common ones. Your guide says you may have some fish later for dinner, depending on the fishers' luck.

An adult and an immature loon swim together on the calm surface of Blue Sea Lake in Quebec, Canada.

BIRDS IN BOREAL FOREST

Almost half of all the bird species in North America use the boreal forest at some point during the year. It's estimated that at least three billion birds (land birds, shorebirds, and water birds) breed in this ecosystem each year. Some other birds, including geese and swans, travel through the boreal forest on their way to breed further north.

As you are heading away from the lake, your guide points out a loon nest. It is made of marsh grasses and sedges that grow around the edge of the lake. It's a good-sized nest—nearly 2 feet (61 cm) across. Male loons choose the site for their nests, usually in a protected and quiet spot by the lakeshore. This nest is empty now. But just a couple of weeks ago, there were two eggs (brown with dark splotches) in it. You're disappointed that you didn't get to see the chicks.

Your guide is leading you through a stand of black spruce trees when you spy a flash of bright pink not too far away. You wander off trail to see what could be so colorful. You crouch down and find a few pink flowers, called lady's slippers. These spectacular flowers are members of the orchid family. The leaves can be up to 8 inches (20 cm) long and are thinly covered with short hairs. Some folks call these flowers moccasin flowers because they resemble the footwear worn by **aboriginal** people. You get out your phone and take a few photos.

Pink lady's slippers are not the only orchids to grow in the taiga. Others are the lesser roundleaf orchid and the northern twayblade. You definitely hope to see more. You mention to your guide that your mom is a huge gardener and that you'd like to surprise her with a few sketches and photographs of the taiga plants. He says he has some ideas.

This pink lady's slipper orchid in bloom is one of several beautiful varieties that decorate the floor of the taiga.

AFTERNOON

YOU approach a clearing in the woods. The sun is higher in the sky now, and you take off your sweatshirt. You dig through your backpack in search of a sunhat. Even though the taiga gets more **precipitation** in summer than in winter, today's forecast looks clear. In July, temperatures in Canada's boreal forest are generally between 59 and 68 degrees Fahrenheit (15 to 20° Celsius). You're really glad to be hiking here in the summer since winter temperatures in the taiga are usually less than 14°F (-10°C).

Even though you ate not too long ago, your belly is starting to growl a bit. It's loud enough that your guide hears it. How embarrassing! But your embarrassment goes away quickly when you are given the chance to look for berries. What an awesome idea! Lucky for you, your guide grew up in this area and knows some of the best spots to find berries. But so do the many other animals—from tiny rodents to large bears—living in the taiga.

Wild bunchberry plants with their bright red fruit grow in a forest in southeast Alaska.

It's not long until you come upon a plant called the bunchberry. You've never seen it before. Dense clusters of small red berries replace this plant's flowers in summertime. Bunchberries can grow in rich or poor soil, as well as in peat moss. Hikers like to munch bunchberries on the trail. Other folks collect them to make sauces, puddings, or preserves. You bite into a berry. Its tiny seeds are crunchy but you find the berry

A brown bear enjoys a summer berry feast in Alaska's Denali National Park.

itself not too exciting. Many people describe bunchberries as tasteless and kind of mealy.

As you hike past a stretch of tamarack trees, you see animal **scat** (poop). Yuck! You are glad you were looking on the ground for berries, or you might have stepped in it. Your guide squats down for a closer look. He says that bears must have been around here in the last couple of days. The scat belongs to them. Your heart beats a little faster knowing that you could have run into a bear if you'd been hunting for berries at a slightly earlier time. These creatures are especially dangerous if surprised by people or when the bears have cubs with them.

Both black bears and grizzly (brown) bears make their homes in Canada's taiga regions. They are omnivores, meaning they eat both plants and animals. Brown bears can weigh 700 pounds (318 kilograms) and be 8 feet (2.4 meters) long. However, these intimidating creatures often eat berries, nuts, fruit, roots, and leaves. That's not to say they don't also eat a variety of animals from fish to moose to rodents. At this time of year, the bears are chowing down and fattening up. They **hibernate** through the taiga's long winter.

Before you can get to the next berry patch, there's a pond your guide wants you to see. He puts his finger over his lips, suggesting you keep quiet. Why? He points at the water's surface. And then you see it—a horned grebe with a chick riding on its back. So cute! The chicks

A horned grebe swims in a pond in south-central Alaska during the summer. Notice that one chick is riding on her back.

can dive and swim as soon as they hatch. But a free ride on its parent's back is nice too. It looks like the mother grebe is eating insects off the water's surface.

Horned grebes are quiet. They tend to be silent unless on their breeding grounds. Then they make a variety of shrieks, croaks, and chattering sounds. You find this bird's appearance to be a bit odd, especially its very noticeable **buff**-colored ear **tufts**. Horned grebes swallow lots of their own feathers. Say what? These birds swallow feathers, enough to make a matted plug of them. These feathers might function as a filter or keep fish bones in their stomachs until they are digested.

Quite a few **aquatic** plants seem to be growing at the edges of this pond. Sedges and pondweeds are just two examples. These plants provide shelter and food for animals here. Migratory waterbirds and shorebirds eat these aquatic plants and distribute their seeds through their waste.

It's just about lunchtime. Not far from the pond is a small clearing. You eat a sandwich and a granola bar. You wonder what you should do with your trash. There's no barrel around. Your guide says that any trash you create must be taken back to a secure, bear-proof container.

A common raven (or northern raven) perches on a tree in its taiga home.

RAVENS

Among the year-round residents of Canada's taiga is the common raven. With their sleek black feathers, ravens are talented and acrobatic fliers. These birds are large, with a wingspan of 44 to 55 inches (1.1 to 1.4 m). Teams of ravens sometimes work together to hunt prey that would be too large for a single bird to take down.

A sedge marsh borders a lake in the taiga of Alberta, Canada. Coniferous trees tower above the sedge in the background.

Wild animals shouldn't eat people's trash or food scraps. You put your wrapper and sandwich bag back in your backpack for now.

Even though you hadn't thought to bring a dessert, it turns out you didn't need one. Very close to your lunch spot is the second berry patch of the day. Score! You had thought your guide might bring you to a place with blueberries. After all, they do grow in the moist soils of the taiga. But instead, you get to try another new fruit—black huckleberries. Native people have long enjoyed black huckleberries. Some people eat them raw. Others enjoy them in muffins, jams, or pies.

Bzzz! A mosquito buzzes around your head. Then comes another and another. Perhaps they smell the handful of berries you are toting around. Slap! You get one. It leaves a bloody spot on your arm. Perhaps you should have worn insect repellent after all.

Just because the taiga is cold in winter doesn't mean that no insects live here. Spruce beetles make their homes in the trees of the boreal forest, which in turn serve as food sources for other animals like woodpeckers. The woodpeckers chisel away at the bark of the taiga's trees to dig out these tasty (to them) creatures.

It's time to head to another section of the taiga. Your guide has more things he wants to show you.

This photo shows a stand of tamarack trees that have turned gold in the autumn. Tamaracks are members of the pine family.

TAMARACK TREES: DECIDUOUS CONIFERS

One of the more unusual trees in the taiga is the tamarack (aka larch). Like other conifers, these trees have needles. But in the autumn, when the weather cools, these needles turn yellow and fall off, much like the leaves of **deciduous** trees. Aboriginal people have used the bark of the tamarack for medicine and its wood to make arrow shafts.

EVENING

EVEN though your guide lives not far from the area you have been visiting, he wants to show you another part of the taiga. So you go back to the cabin and get his jeep. You drive along winding roads with very few cars. There are towns throughout Canada's boreal forest areas. Overall, the feeling is one of nature and not development.

Shortly after you get out of the car, you notice that some of the trees here look misshapen or stunted. The short growing season of the taiga, plus the winter exposure to ice and snow, can deform the trees. In fact, scientists have measured the age of trees that are only a few feet tall and found some to be 150 years old! You see some shrubby-looking black spruce that fit this description. Your guide tells you that muskrats, moose, and mink are just a few of the animals that live in this kind of **habitat**. Some of the shrubs and trees in the area have been munched by moose until they are stunted. Your guide says this is called "moose browse."

Continuous exposure to fierce winds has deformed the branches of this white spruce.

Moose are the largest **herbivores** found in Canada's taiga. The largest members of the deer family, moose can stand taller than a man and weigh up to 1,800 pounds (828 kg). They eat a variety of plants in the taiga. They often use their enormous hooves to dig around on the forest floor in search of **lichens** and mosses to eat.

A bull moose feeds on aquatic vegetation in British Columbia, Canada. An adult moose eats up to 26 pounds (12 kilograms) of food per day in the summer.

In the summer, moose also eat aquatic plants. These creatures are super-powerful. A kick from their giant hooves could kill a person. Moose are known for being good swimmers. You imagine how cool it would be to see a gigantic moose out for a swim.

You follow a narrow trail to a bog. Your guide points out several different plants. Cotton grass grows well in the bog's acidic soil. Its fluffy white seed heads look like cotton and disperse easily in the wind. You like the name of a plant called Labrador tea. This evergreen shrub is about four feet

A field of Arctic cotton grass blooms in the summer sunshine in Canada. The Inuit use cotton grass as a wick in their lamps.

This insectivorous northern pitcher plant has caught a bug in its trap. The plant is located in a bog in Michigan.

tall with big, white, five-petaled flowers. During the American War of Independence, people used its leaves to make tea.

Of all the plants you see near this bog, you think the pitcher plant is the most fascinating. These plants get their name from the jug-shaped vessel created by some of its leaves. Pitcher plants are carnivorous, or meat-eating. Sounds strange, right? Insect-eating plants often grow well in peat bogs. Since these areas have little oxygen and few nutrients, carnivorous plants can get extra nutrients from trapping and digesting insects.

How does the process work? This amazing plant secretes nectar at the top of its pitcher, which is filled with water. Insects are attracted to the nectar. They slide down the pitcher and drown. The plant contains bacteria that decompose the insects. Then the plant absorbs whatever nutrients are released from their bodies.

As you are taking a picture of the pitcher plant, you hear the sound of frogs. The sound reminds you of when you run your finger along the teeth of a comb. They are boreal chorus frogs. These tiny frogs reach a maximum length of only about 1.5 inches (4 cm). They can be brown to greenish-gray. They also have a white stripe along the upper lip and a dark stripe through the eye. These little frogs feed on insects and other **invertebrates**.

There aren't that many varieties of **amphibians** in the taiga. The climate is too harsh for these cold-blooded creatures. Some animals, including the boreal chorus frog, can

DECIDUOUS TREES IN THE BOREAL FOREST

Even though most of the trees in the taiga are conifers, there are some deciduous trees as well. These trees are adapted to the taiga's harsh conditions. For example, the aspen has **chlorophyll** in its bark, which lets it make some food on warmer winter days. Birch, balsam poplar, and trembling aspen trees are spread widely through the boreal forest. They take nutrients from leaves before shedding them, and use these nutrients for growing the next year.

A patch of boreal forest has been clear-cut in British Columbia, Canada.

CLEAR-CUTTING THE TAIGA

A major threat to the taiga is the cutting of its trees. Clear-cutting is the most common type of logging in the taiga. It involves cutting all of the trees in an area. Cutting boreal forests takes away animals' homes and breaks up their habitats. Clear-cutting can also lead to **erosion,** where the taiga's soil can be blown away by wind or carried off by water.

survive by hibernating in the winter. They might hibernate beneath logs or under the ground. However, at this time of year, the boreal chorus frogs eat insects and call to their fellow frogs.

The wood frog is another hardy animal of the taiga. In the warmer weather, the wood frog breeds and eats. The diet of these frogs includes insects and worms. They have to look out for predators like birds, foxes, and raccoons. In the winter, the wood frog has some amazing adaptations to survive the cold. Its body produces a substance similar to the antifreeze that is in your car. This substance prevents the wood frog's whole body from turning to ice and causing it to freeze to death. During this time, the wood frog-sicle (like a frog popsicle) stops breathing. Its heart stops beating. And when the weather warms up, the wood frog thaws out—good as new!

The air is starting to cool as the sun is getting lower in the sky. You need your sweatshirt again. You start hiking along a slightly wider trail. On a

A boreal chorus frog blends in among the leaf litter of its habitat. These frogs rarely live longer than three years.

A red fox leaps with its eyes focused on prey in its forest home. These animals are solitary hunters.

whim, you decide to get your phone out for its camera. It seems like you never can tell when you might have a wildlife sighting. Not more than ten minutes later, your hunch proves right. Just a little off the trail you see a red fox. It's not too big, so it must be a young fox. It has orange-red fur on its sides, back, and head, and white fur on its chest and under its neck. Its bushy tail is easy to spot.

The fox looks to be chasing a rodent of some sort. Your guide says it's a taiga vole. You get out your binoculars quickly for a better look. The vole has reddish-brown fur. It's rather plump and is just over 8 inches (20 cm) long. The fox pounces and catches the vole. Dinnertime for the fox. Thinking of dinner, you hope you'll have yours soon.

NIGHT

YOUR guide says that pretty soon you will arrive at a tourist lodge located near a small lake in the taiga. The light is getting dimmer. All of a sudden, your foot falls into a hole you didn't see. You twist your ankle a bit. Ouch!

Since you started hiking this morning, you've noticed the uneven ground in the taiga. Large sections of the taiga contain **permafrost**, which is a layer of permanently frozen soil that lies beneath the soil you're stepping on. In other parts of the taiga, there's a layer of bedrock just under the soil. Rock and permafrost both prevent water from draining out of the soil's top layers. That's why there are so many muskegs in the taiga—the water has nowhere to go, so it stays in the top layers of the ground. You would have had very wet feet many times today if you hadn't worn your rubber boots.

Several whitefish are supported by aquatic plants on the water's surface after being caught by a fisher.

Luckily, it's not too far to the lodge. You arrive and put your foot up on a bench overlooking the lake. You smell fish cooking on a grill. The women working at the lodge caught some lake whitefish this afternoon. These fish are known for being hard to catch. They can also be large, weighing 20 pounds (9 kg) or more. Your guide looks impressed. He also says that lake whitefish are delicious.

An American mink scans its surroundings in its Minnesota home. These minks are territorial and will fight others that invade their territory.

While you are waiting for the fish to cook, you hear "hoo hoo!" And like a flash, a great-horned owl swoops down from a nearby tree and grabs something in its powerful talons. You can't tell if its prey is a small raccoon or a squirrel. You ask your guide. He says the owl has caught a mink.

Mink have long and sleek bodies but stubby, short legs. Their brown-to-black fur is really soft and is covered with special guard hairs that make

Many of the trees in this forest in Idaho have been damaged by spruce budworms. These insects eat the trees' needles and new shoots.

their coats waterproof. Mink are carnivores. They eat a range of foods including mice, fish, frogs, and birds. They kill their prey by biting it on the neck. This time, the mink was prey for the owl!

A man sitting nearby on the deck says he once made the mistake of intruding on a mink's den in the late spring. It sprayed a foul-smelling liquid all over him. Mink can't aim their spray and just hope the nasty odor will drive predators away. Phew!

Finally, your dinner is ready. The whitefish is delicious, just as promised. And for dessert, you are served a delicious huckleberry and blueberry pie made with fresh-picked berries.

Since it's getting too dark for hiking on uneven ground, your guide offers you a nighttime canoe ride. He has a lantern on board and is planning to stay close to shore. You see a number of moths flitting about. You wonder if any of them are spruce budworms.

The river otter is quite sensitive to environmental pollution.

These native insects have been one of the most damaging pests to affect the spruce and true fir trees of Canada. Spruce budworms defoliate the trees they live in, which can kill enormous stands of forest (millions of acres).

Across the lake, you hear some splashing. Your guide aims the lantern in that direction. What is causing the commotion? It's an otter hunting for food. It uses its powerful tail and webbed feet to propel it through the water. These excellent swimmers can hold their breath underwater for as long as eight minutes. Otters have ears and nostrils that can close when they are in the water. While they do eat amphibians, fish are their preferred food. They hunt more at night in the warm months, but during the day in winter.

When you return to the lodge, you hear a loud noise. It sounds like metal crashing. Suddenly, the women who cooked your dinner rush down the lodge's steps to where the garbage cans are stored. A family of raccoons

Gray wolves work together when looking for a meal.

WOLVES

Another **nocturnal** animal in the taiga is the gray wolf. The largest members of the dog family, these wolves can weigh 40 to 175 pounds (18 to 79 kg). Gray wolves are carnivores. They hunt in packs. They work together to take down prey such as deer, moose, and elk.

An angry wolverine bares its teeth. A wolverine may roam 15 miles (24 km) per day in search of food.

has been having a party. Several of these masked bandits managed to get into a couple of the cans. Using their long fingers and dexterous paws, these clever creatures pulled out their own feast. After all, they are fattening up before they spend a chunk of the winter asleep in their den. You notice two other raccoons getting a drink from the lake. Then the group, known as a nursery, takes off into the woods.

Before you head to bed, your guide tells you about one more nocturnal animal—the wolverine. In all his years living in the taiga, he has only seen one once in the wild. He says it was rather terrifying. A wolverine looks like a small bear and is 26 to 36 inches long (66 to 91 cm), not counting its tail. They belong to the weasel family.

The wolverine's scientific name, *Gulo gulo*, comes from the Latin word that means "glutton." Wolverines have enormous appetites and are known for being fierce. These predators can take down prey five times larger than they are. They will not hesitate to fight bears or wolves for their food. Wolverines have razor-sharp teeth and will eat everything from rodents and hares to small bears and deer. Their twenty toes have very sharp claws.

Even though you think it might have been cool to see a wolverine in the wild, your guide's description of seeing one devour its prey makes you glad perhaps you didn't.

There's no way you could see all the amazing plants and animals of the taiga in one day. You fall asleep dreaming of your next round of adventures in this amazing ecosystem.

Siberian tigers roam in their taiga home. They are the world's largest cats.

EUROPEAN AND ASIAN TAIGA

Canada is not the only area with taiga. There is a stretch of taiga across Scandinavia (Finland, Sweden, and Norway). However, Russia has the largest area of taiga on Earth. It stretches from the Pacific Ocean to the Ural Mountains, a distance of about 3,600 miles (5,800 km). Russia's taiga areas are home to reindeer and even Siberian tigers.

WHERE IS THE TAIGA?

The areas highlighted in blue on this map show where the taiga is located.

FAST FACTS ABOUT THE TAIGA

SIZE: Taiga regions vary in size around the globe. Canada's taiga regions take up about 661,500 square miles (1,713,000 square kilometers). This is roughly the size of Alaska.

LOCATION: Most taiga regions are located between latitude 50° and 60° north. They are all in the Northern Hemisphere. In North America. There are large stretches of taiga in Alaska and across Canada. Taiga is also found in Scandinavia and across Russia. Canada's taiga region stretches from the Yukon in the west to Newfoundland and Labrador in the east.

CLIMATE: In some of Canada's taiga region, the mean temperatures average between 59°F and 68°F (15°C to 20°C) in July and less than 14°F (-10°C) in January. Summers are characterized by fifty to one hundred frost-free days. Taiga regions located in the center of continents typically receive 12 to 20 inches (30 to 50 cm) of precipitation per year. But the taiga in eastern North America and northern Europe can get more than 39 inches (100 cm) of precipitation annually. Precipitation is more common in summer.

PLANTS: There are many kinds of plants found in the Canadian taiga. Trees include pines, spruces, firs, tamarack, poplar, and birch. Flowering plants include cloudberry, Labrador tea, and several species of orchids. Aquatic plants include pondweed and sedges. There are also shrubs, grasses, lichens, and mosses.

ANIMALS FOUND IN CANADA'S TAIGA: Amphibians include boreal chorus frogs and wood frogs. Birds include bald eagles, grebes, killdeer, loons, owls, ptarmigans, and woodpeckers. Fish include minnows, whitefish, lake trout, burbot, northern pike, salmon, and yellow perch. Insects include spruce beetles, mosquitoes, and spruce budworms. Mammals include beavers, ermines, wolverines, red fox, black and brown bears, gray wolves, moose, raccoons, snowshoe hares, weasels, and taiga voles.

WATER SOURCES: There are more than 1.5 million lakes in Canada's boreal forests, such as Lake Winnipeg and Reindeer Lake. Rivers include the Peace River and the North Saskatchewan River.

GLOSSARY

aboriginal Inhabiting or existing in a land from before the arrival of colonists; indigenous.

amphibian An annimal that can live both in water and on land, such as frogs and salamanders.

aquatic Living in, growing in, or often found in water.

bog Wet, spongy ground; a poorly drained area where dead plant matter accumulates and sphagnum moss grows in abundance.

boreal Relating to the climatic zone south of the Arctic, particularly the cold temperate region dominated by forests of birch, poplar, and conifers.

buff A yellowish-beige color.

camouflage An animal's natural form or coloring which allows it to blend in with its surroundings.

chlorophyll A green pigment in plants that absorbs light to provide energy for photosynthesis.

conifer A tree that bears cones and has evergreen needlelike or scalelike leaves.

deciduous Shedding its leaves annually, as of a shrub or tree.

ecosystem A community made up of living things interacting with their physical environment.

erosion The process of wearing away by the action of wind, water, or glacial ice.

habitat The place or kind of place where an animal or plant normally lives or grows.

herbivore An animal that eats plants.

hibernate To spend the winter in a resting or sleeping state.

invertebrate An animal lacking a backbone.

larva The young wingless form (like a grub or caterpillar) that hatches from the egg of many insects.

lichen A slow-growing, simple plant that usually forms a low crustlike or leaflike growth on walls, rocks, and trees.

migrate To move from one region or climate to another usually on a regular schedule for breeding or feeding.

muskeg A North American bog or swamp made up of a mixture of water and partially decayed vegetation, often covered by a layer of mosses.

nocturnal A plant or animal active at night.

permafrost A permanently frozen layer of soil below the surface in very cold regions.

photosynthesis The process by which green plants use sunlight to make food from water and carbon dioxide.

precipitation The water which falls to the earth as rain, snow, hail, mist, or sleet.

prey An animal that is hunted or killed by another animal for food.

scat The feces (poop) deposited by an animal.

sedge A plant that's related to the grasses which are found in marshy areas. Sedges often have three-sided stems.

species A group of living organisms made up of similar individuals capable of producing fertile offspring.

tuft A small cluster of grass, hair, or feathers that are attached or close together at the base but free at the opposite end.

FIND OUT MORE

Books

Franchino, Vicky. *Canadian Taiga*. North Mankato, MN: Cherry Lake Publishing, 2016.

Grady, Colin. *The Coniferous Forest Biome*. New York: Enslow Publishing, 2016.

Johansson, Philip. *The Taiga: Discover This Forested Biome*. New York: Enslow Elementary, 2015.

Websites

BBC: Taiga

http://www.bbc.co.uk/nature/habitats/Taiga

This website shows where taigas are found around the world, as well as giving examples of the plants and animals found here. It also has video and sound clips from taigas in different locations.

Canadian Wildlife Federation: Boreal Forest.

http://www.hww.ca/en/wild-spaces/boreal-forest.html

This website focuses mainly on the boreal forests of Canada. It describes the plants and animals of this biome, as well as the benefits of and threats to boreal forests.

National Geographic: Taiga

http://nationalgeographic.org/encyclopedia/taiga

This website explains what taigas are, where they are located, and what threats exist to these ecosystems. It also has lots of photos of taigas and some fun facts.

INDEX

Page numbers in **boldface** are illustrations.

ABOUT THE AUTHOR

From circus science to vampires, **Alicia Klepeis** loves to research fun and out-of-the-ordinary topics that make nonfiction exciting for readers. Alicia began her career at the National Geographic Society. She is the author of numerous children's books including *Bizarre Things We've Called Medicine, Goblins, Understanding Saudi Arabia Today*, and *The World's Strangest Foods*. Alicia is currently working on several projects involving unusual animals, American history, and paranormal experiences. She has not been to the taiga yet but has added it to her list of places to see. Alicia lives with her family in upstate New York.

PHOTO CREDITS